Angels & Ducats

Shakespeare's money & medals

Mr. WILIAM
SHAKESPEARES
COMEDIES
HISTORIES, &
TRAGEDIES,

Publiſhed according to the True Originall Copies.

Martin Droeshout ſculpſit London

LO

Printed by Iſaac Iaggard

Angels & Ducats

Shakespeare's money & medals

Barrie Cook

THE BRITISH MUSEUM PRESS

This book is dedicated to my sisters Deborah and Philippa, with much love. Multiples of sisters do not get a good press in Shakespeare, going by *Macbeth* and *King Lear*. My experience has been rather different.

Barrie Cook has asserted the right to be identified as the author of this work.

First published in 2012 by The British Museum Press
A division of The British Museum Company Ltd
38 Russell Square, London WC1B 3QQ
britishmuseum.org/publishing

A catalogue record for this book is available from the British Library.

ISBN 978-0-7141-1821-5

Designed by Caroline and Roger Hillier, The Old Chapel Graphic Design
www.theoldchapelivinghoe.com
Printed in China by C&C Offset Printing Co. Ltd.

The majority of the objects featured in this book are from the collection of the British Museum. Their museum registration numbers are listed on page 95. Further information about the Museum and its collection can be found at britishmuseum.org.

Frontispiece: Title page of the First Folio, 1623.
Engraving, H 32 cm, W 21.8 cm. Stonyhurst College, Lancashire.
And, group of Elizabethan and Jacobean gold coins. British Museum, London.

Contents

This yellow slave

What is here?

Gold? Yellow, glittering, precious gold?

No, gods, I am no idle votarist;

Roots, you clear heavens. Thus much of this will make

Black white, foul fair, wrong right,

Base noble, old young, coward valiant.

Ha, you gods! Why this? What's this, you gods? Why, this

Will lug your priests and servants from your sides,

Pluck stout men's pillows from below their heads:

This yellow slave

Will knit and break religions, bless th'accursed,

Make the hoar leprosy adored, place thieves

And give them title, knee and approbation

With senators on the bench. This is it

That makes the wappened widow wed again;

She whom the spittle house and ulcerous sores

Would cast the gorge at, this embalms and spices

To th'April day again. Come, damnèd earth,

Thou common whore of mankind, that puts odds

Among the rout of nations, I will make thee

Do thy right nature.

(*Timon of Athens*, 4.3.25 – 45)

Group of
Elizabethan and
Jacobean gold coins.
British Museum,
London

Paeans of ironic praise to the power of money are not rare in English Renaissance literature, if not always as sulphurous as the rant of the ruined Timon, finding a hoard of gold while scrabbling for roots in a forest. 'Thou visible god', Timon goes on to call gold (4.3.389), and it is probably no surprise that this passage was a favourite of Karl Marx.

The plays of William Shakespeare (1564–1616) are full of references to money in general and coins in particular. For Shakespeare, and indeed other playwrights of the age, money was a recognizable and ubiquitous part of everyday life and it was also – and consequently – a fertile source of metaphor in dramatic verse and comic dialogue, as these illuminate fundamental questions of authenticity and identity, legacy and morality. Purses and persons and ducats and daughters mix inextricably 'in money and in love' – and that is only in *The Merchant of Venice* (1.1.133). Coins are used to give crucial information on status and character, as plot devices and to add local colour, but also as a means of engaging with profound issues. Shakespeare makes much less use of medals, since these were only beginning to be used in England in any numbers during his lifetime, but he was aware of this expanding art form.

This book is far from the first attempt to engage with Shakespeare's monetary references. Numismatists bring their knowledge of coins to bear, while historians and literary scholars use the results to explore text and context, money in Shakespeare's mind, works and world. This contribution makes the best use the author is able of this accumulated scholarship, to support and develop an exhibition held at the British Museum in 2012. It could easily be bigger; but, as a curator of coins, my professional career rests on the assumption that small things can still have an interest.

Note on the monetary system of early modern England
Throughout this period English money was usually reckoned in £sd, pounds, shillings and pence: the pound of 20 shillings and the shilling of 12 pence (so 240 pennies to the pound). As a unit of money, the history of the pound sterling from Shakespeare's day to our own is continuous and unbroken, unlike the penny, which is now 100 to the pound. Many early modern coins had individual names (noble, angel, crown, groat), but also had a specific valuation in £sd.

Chapter 1

He that wears her like a medal

Images of power and allegiance

Why, he that wears her like a medal, hanging
About his neck, Bohemia
(*The Winter's Tale*, 1.2.354-5)

The word medal occurs just once in the entire Shakespearean corpus, in these words from *The Winter's Tale*. Soon after John Webster would follow, in *The Duchess of Malfi*, describing the Duchess and her corrupted siblings: 'You never fix'd your eye on three fair medals,/ cast in one figure, of so

Title-page of the
Bishops' Bible from
the quarto edition,
1569
Printed on vellum
and hand-coloured,
H 21.5 cm, W 16 cm
British Library,
London

different temper' (1.1.188–9). Largely an Italian invention, medals were a widespread art form in much of Europe by the late sixteenth century, but the number of examples made in England was small and the number made by English artists smaller. However, things were beginning to change and a major native figure, the miniaturist Nicholas Hilliard, collaborated with engravers in work on medals as well as coins and seals. In the early seventeenth century English travellers, especially to Italy, began to accumulate medal collections to emulate gentlemen scholars on the continent. Medals provided memorials of individuals and events, usually explicitly (at least for the Latinate), but explicit or otherwise, they offer almost without exception images of power.

The most familiar images of power and authority from English and British history are arguably sixteenth century: iconic representations of Henry VIII and Elizabeth I. These were not images confined to paintings covering half a palace wall or delicate miniatures in the cabinets of the elite. This is, for the first time, an age of mass-produced images accessible to the population at large. Printing brought images and words together and at a price affordable to ever larger sections of society. A book or broadsheet with woodcut illustrations might not have the opulent beauty of an illuminated manuscript, but they were a fraction of the cost. From 1568 Elizabeth I looked out from every copy of the *Bishops' Bible*, supposedly in every church and many a home.

Coins and medals were also mass-produced objects, vehicles for the depiction of authority, inscribed with realistic

portraits of rulers for the first time since classical antiquity. Everyone in Tudor and Stuart England could hold in the hand an image that, more or less flatteringly, gave them a sense of the monarch as an individual, of who their ruler was as a person as well as an office or name.

Throughout Shakespeare's own life, one image dominated: that of Elizabeth I, viewable in every monetary transaction. A major recoinage in 1560 meant that little older coin remained in currency thereafter. Only with the accession of James I in 1603 did a second image join that of 'the late queen of famous memory', a mature, bearded man in armour. James's own issues never came anywhere near eclipsing those of Elizabeth in the accumulated English currency (it was, of course, different in Scotland, which kept its own monetary system), but his coins were perhaps designedly different, with their overtly militant character. In some ways this is surprising. James usually promoted a personal image as peacemaker and wise man over warrior and conqueror – Solomon not David, Augustus not Julius Caesar. However, coinage was one medium in which the fundamental difference between masculine and feminine power – the ability to lead in war (however notionally) – was strongly manifested in a very clear way.

Medals and counters could not compete with the sheer ubiquity of coins, though they had merits of their own. They could spread a wider range of images and be souvenirs of the more extended Stuart royal family (Queen Anne; Henry, the new Prince of Wales; Princess Elizabeth; and Prince Charles), a contrast to

Medallion
of Maximilian,
Archduke of Austria,
brother of the
current king
of Bohemia, *c.* 1612
Gold and enamel,
L 8.8 cm, W 5.2 cm
British Museum,
London

Elizabeth's solitary majesty and the promise of a more secure future with a clear line of succession.

Medals also indicated allegiance and friendship, patronage and respect and it is this aspect that brings us to the context of Shakespeare's single medal reference, made in 1611. The scene is a royal court, of Sicilia, where the paranoid King Leontes convinces himself that his queen Hermione is having an affair with the visiting Polixenes, King of Bohemia. He agitatedly describes Hermione greeting Polixenes as a medal hanging around his neck. This in itself shows a specific perception of a medal, more like a pendant than a modern commemorative medal, which is not worn at all, or a military decoration, pinned to the chest. Shakespeare is familiar with medals hanging like this and expects his audience to be also.

These medals, often with loops to permit their suspension from a chain or ribbon, were essentially mass-produced equivalents of portrait miniatures. One of the first great examples is the 'Dangers Averted' medal of Elizabeth, produced probably in 1589, after the defeat of the Armada, a classic depiction of the queen in triumph. However, English medals only really began to proliferate under James I. He was the first English monarch to produce a medal for his coronation, accompanied by one for Queen Anne of Denmark, small, silver ones to be scattered at points in the ceremony. A medal with a loop commemorated the peace treaty with Spain signed in 1604, and we know Shakespeare was probably in attendance at its ceremonial signing in the Chapel Royal.

Shakespeare would have had many opportunities to see such medals on his appearances at court as

Dangers Averted
medal of Queen
Elizabeth I, 1589
Cast and chased
gold, Diam. 4.4 cm
British Museum,
London

Peace with Spain
medal, 1604
Gold, Diam. 3.7 cm
British Museum,
London

King James I signing
a treaty with Spain
in the Chapel Royal,
1623
Woodcut on paper,
H 27.3 cm, W 32.4 cm
British Museum,
London

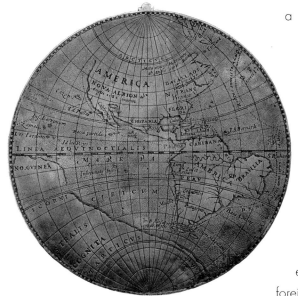

a performer, especially during the crowded entertainments of the Christmas season, when his playing company alone might have performed half a dozen plays. Midway through the festivities, on 1 January, came the day on which seasonal gifts were given and at the Jacobean court gold medals on chains were a prominent part of this, especially to the representatives of foreign royalty. In 1605, for example, the new year's gifts included: to a messenger of the Elector Palatine, 'one cheyne of gold and one medaillie of gold with the king's picture therein'; the departing Spanish ambassador received from Queen Anne 'one chayne of gold and one medall of gold with the Queene's picture on the one side and the Prince's on the other, with a border of diamonds about yt'; while the Danish, Polish and Venetian ambassadors also received chains and medals of gold.

With this in mind, we can see Leontes' fevered mind turning his queen into a medal, no longer belonging to him, but to an imagined rival; not a harmless trinket around the neck, but a cruel sign of betrayal.

Cast silver medal depicting the circumnavigation voyage of Sir Francis Drake, by Michael Mercator, 1589
Silver, Diam. 6.7 cm
British Museum, London

Other medals of the time, whether or not Shakespeare knew them, illuminate the world he was part of. One medal, indeed, actually depicts that world with astonishing clarity. It was a newly expanding and newly-familiar world, as in the last years of Elizabeth's reign English mariners and explorers began to compete seriously with the Spanish, Portuguese and Dutch. Francis Drake circumnavigated the globe between 1577 and 1580, and a medal of 1589 recorded his discoveries, each side showing a hemisphere with the voyage picked out across successive oceans. It was a map in silver, a globe in two dimensions. Encompassing the world was now a topical subject, and both Puck and Oberon play with the idea in *A Midsummer Night's Dream*: 'We the globe can compass soon,/ Swifter than the wand'ring moon' (4.1.89–90). Walter Ralegh's Guiana expeditions inspire Falstaff's visions of seducing and exploiting the two Merry Wives of Windsor (1.3.47–50):

she is a region in Guiana,
all gold and bounty. I will be
cheaters to them both, and
they shall be exchequers to me.
They shall be my East and West
Indies, and I will trade to them both.

Shakespeare knows all about the brave new world and how it was represented. The first English-made three-dimensional globes appeared in 1592 and get referenced very quickly in *The Comedy of Errors* (3.2.104-5, 119-22), in a description of Nell, the rotund maid-servant, that veers off into a comic version of the Spanish empire:

Dromio of Syracuse:

No longer from head to foot than from hip to hip;

she is spherical, like a globe;

I could find out countries in her...

Antipholus of Syracuse:

Where America, the Indies?

Dromio of Syracuse:

Oh, sir, upon her nose all o'er embellished with rubies, carbuncles, sapphires, declining their rich aspect to the hot breath of Spain; who sent whole armadoes of caracks to be ballast at her nose.

When Shakespeare's company built its own new theatre in Southwark, it was named the Globe, presenting the world to view in its own way.

III

From an enlarged Drawing of an extensive View of London, in 1647. 7 Feet 9 Inches, by 18 Inches, engraved by Hollar, very scarce, and now in the Possession of Thomas Lloyd Esq.

THE GLOBE THEATRE.

This structure must have been erected previous to the year 1563, as it is represented in a Plan of London, published during that year, but excluded in another plan published from actual survey, in 1600, though it is known that many of Shakspeare's plays were performed in it at subsequent periods.— Stow records the destruction of this Theatre, during the year 1613, in a particular manner. He says, "Upon St Peters day last, the playhouse or theater, called the Globe, upon the Banck-side, neere London, by negligent discharging of a peale of ordnance, close to the South Side thereof, the Thatch tooke fier, and the wind sodainly desperst the flame round about, and in a very short space the whole building was quite consumed, and no man hurt. The house being filled with people, to behold the play, viz. of Henry the 8." And the next Spring it was new builded in far fairer manner then before.— Ben Jonson calls the Globe Theatre, the "Glory of the Bank, and the Fort of the whole parish."

London, Published Oct.ª 20ᵗʰ 1810, by Robᵗ Williamson, Nº 58 Cornhill.

Bird's-eye view of Southwark looking towards the Globe Theatre, after Wenceslaus Hollar, 1810
Etching and engraving on paper, H 27.5 cm, W 20.9 cm
British Museum, London

Chapter 2

Thou pale and common drudge 'tween man and man

The costs of theatre

Did not Will Summers break his wind for thee?
And Shakespeare therefore write his comedy?
All things acknowledge thy vast power divine
(Great God of Money) whose most powerful shine
Gives motion, life.

(Thomas Randolph, *Hey for Honesty*, 1627)

Long View of London, by Wenceslaus Hollar, 1647 showing the Globe Theatre, mislabelled the bear-baiting arena, on the south bank of the river Thames. Etching, H 46.6 cm, W 39 cm British Museum, London

*T*his quote from a seventeenth-century play links Will Summers, Henry VIII's jester, and Will Shakespeare, undisputed titan of the theatre – low comedy and dramatic genius, all dependent on money. True enough. Shakespeare and his generation invented the commercial theatre in Britain, venues accessible to all for a fee and open all the year round, at least in the capital city. Shakespeare invested his time and his talents as actor and writer in this new venture and left it a rich man.

In the theatrical world of the late Elizabethan age there were two leading acting companies in London. They were essentially owned and run by the core actors and Shakespeare was one of these. As both actor and chief writer, he was one of the eight men (later twelve) running the Lord Chamberlain's Men, under the patronage of one great Elizabethan courtier, Lord Hunsdon, the queen's close relative on the Boleyn side. Their, perhaps friendly, rivals were the Lord Admiral's Men, under the patronage of another cousin of the queen, the Earl of Nottingham. Following the queen's death in 1603, Shakespeare's company received the direct patronage of the new monarch, James I, and became the King's Men based at the Globe in Southwark. The Admiral's Men, at the Fortune Theatre near Cripplegate, transferred to the heir to the throne, Prince Henry, and in 1605–6 a third company, Queen Anne's Men (formerly Worcester's Men) settled at the Red Bull in Clerkenwell.

Attending a play by Shakespeare at one of London's large, open-air theatres – in Shoreditch the Theatre or the

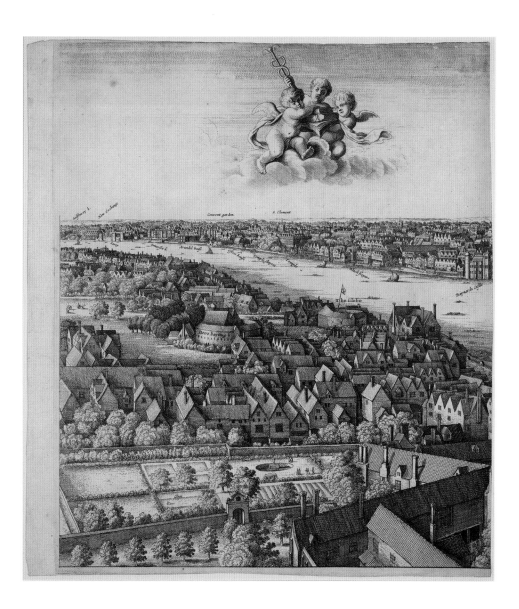

Drawing of the Swan
Theatre in London,
by Arendt van Buchell
after a sketch by Joannes
de Witt, after 1596-7
Pen and brown ink on
paper, H 19.8 cm, W 15.8 cm
Utrecht University
Library, Utrecht

Group of silver coins
in increasing denominations:
Halfpenny of Elizabeth I,
1597-90, Diam. 0.8 cm;
Penny of James I, 1609-10,
Diam. 1.3 cm; Penny of
Elizabeth I, 1589-92,
Diam. 1.3 cm; Half-groat
(twopence) of Elizabeth I,
1594-6, Diam. 1.7 cm; Groat
(fourpence) of Mary I,
1554-5, Diam. 2.4 cm;
Sixpence of Elizabeth I,
1591, Diam. 2.6 cm;
Shilling of James I, 1607,
Diam. 3.1 cm;
British Museum, London

Curtain, in Southwark the Rose, the Swan or, from 1599, the new Globe – was to enter the commercial world with a vengeance. 'Behold the sumptuous Theatre-houses, a continual monument of London's prodigality and folly', a preacher at St Paul's declaimed in 1577. Money-making was the point of their creation: no more passing the hat in uncontrolled market places or inn-yards. Payment was upfront and compulsory. But this also meant ensuring audience satisfaction, a production-line of new plays to encourage repeat business and keep several playhouses in profit.

Money was needed everywhere in a theatre visit and the afternoon's excursion to the theatre floated on a sea of silver, 'thou pale and common drudge/ 'Tween man and man', as Bassanio describes it in the *Merchant of Venice* (3.2.105–6). If you wanted to cross the river to go to the Globe, the Rose or the Swan on the South Bank and London Bridge – the only bridge over the Thames – was not convenient, you paid one of the many watermen fourpence or sixpence for passage. Next you paid the so-called 'gatherers' for admission. First nights generally cost twice as much as ordinary performances. At the Globe it was a penny to stand in the yard in front of the stage; it then cost another penny to move to actual seats in the balcony ('the twopenny gallery') and a third penny to get to the upper galleries with cushions and the best stage views. The playwright Thomas Dekker joked about 'the Two-peny Clients and Peny Stinkards' in the hierarchy of theatre-goers. The upper classes, meanwhile, had private galleries that cost sixpence or more, with their own outside staircases, to avoid squeezing

through the common sort. Modern excavations at the Globe and Rose theatres produced large numbers of ceramic money-boxes, presumably used by the 'gatherers' and by refreshment sellers. Very few coins were excavated, however – the clean-up operation was extremely thorough it seems and lost coins did not stay lost.

At the smaller indoor theatres, like the King's Men's Blackfriars, the geography of spectatorship was a little different, the audience smaller and charges higher: sixpence to get in and watch from the upper gallery; a shilling to sit on a bench in the pit; two shillings to sit on the stage itself and half a crown (2s.6d.) for one of the expensive gallery boxes. The prologue to *Henry VIII* in 1612 is probably referencing a Blackfriars' performance (9‑13):

Chorus:

> Those that come to see
> Only a show or two, and so agree
> The play may pass. If they be still and willing
> I'll undertake may see away their shilling
> Richly in two short hours.

Detail of Hollar's *Long View* of London showing Blackfriars

In *Henry IV Part 1* Falstaff's pockets hold nothing but 'tavern-reck'nings, memorandums of bawdy-houses, and one poor penny-worth of sugar-candy' (3.3.116‑17). And you could buy a broadsheet ballad for a penny, so a theatre visit cost no more than a snack and a magazine. Theatre was affordable and frequent visits perfectly possible, perhaps more like the cinema today.

The cost of items in Shakespeare's time

Going to the theatre

Crossing the Thames by boat	4d.-6d.
Entry to the Globe yard	1d.
Entry to the Globe lower galleries	2d.
Entry to the Globe upper galleries	3d.
Entry to the Globe boxes	12d. (shilling)
Entry to the Blackfriars gallery	6d.
Entry to the Blackfriars pit	12d. (shilling)
Entry to Blackfriars box	2s.6d. (half a crown)

Income and expenses

Estimate of English crown revenues in 1600	£591,000
Estimated annual profits of the Globe Theatre	£1,200
Shakespeare's estimated annual income from Globe profits	£40
Range of payments for plays	£5-£12
Cost of high status costume	£6
Estimated annual salary of salaried actors and hired men	£10-£15
Estimated annual salary of labourer	£10
Annual income on which a gentleman could live	£40
Cost of a play published in quarto	6d.
Cost of the 1623 First Folio (unbound)	£1

Thanks to the accidents of documentary survival, we do not have much detailed financial information for Shakespeare's own company. But we do have for their rivals, the Lord Admiral's Men, in the shape of records of the theatrical entrepreneur Philip Henslowe. His accounts are the source for most of the prices in this chapter. There was no such thing as an average year, but one estimate suggests that the annual gross income of the Globe in its heyday was probably something like £1,200: costs ran at about £420, leaving profit for the company members. Most of them, including Shakespeare, would have taken away about £40 a year (there were different levels of investment so not everyone took the same percentage). Additionally, Shakespeare would probably have been paid for his new plays, as well as earning from the custom of the writer receiving the profits from the second or third performance as a sort of benefit.

Henslowe's accounts tell us that playwrights working for the Admiral's Men were paid between £5 and £8 for a play, rising to £10 or £12 after 1600, about the annual income of a labourer. While we do not know details of Shakespeare's playwriting income during his life, the habit of ring-fencing the second-night profits of a new or revived play continued and after his death the company made other use of the money in ways that are recorded. So we know that the performance of *Othello* on 22 November 1629 brought in second night profits of £9 16s. and *Richard II* on 12 June 1631 brought in £5 6s.6d. The author's benefit performance could virtually double his income from a play. Shakespeare may also have been paid for writing additional material for his own and other authors' plays for revivals, performances at court, revisions and so on. His annual income could easily have been in the £100 bracket or more. Meanwhile, the salaried minor actors were paid 10s a week and probably only half that on tour, maybe £10 to £15 a year. It was estimated at the time that a moderate gentleman could live on £40 a year, so, with his income and the land-holdings and investments he was able to acquire, Shakespeare became extremely prosperous. His position as stake-holder in the company was vital in this – most contemporary writers for the stage, living purely by the pen (Lyly, Peele, Kyd, Nashe, Dekker – even Ben Jonson), ended their days in comparative or absolute poverty.

In theory, the players performed most days through the year, except Sundays and during Lent; the death of a member of the royal family closed the theatres as did, more frequently, outbreaks of the plague, which sent the players fleeing into the less profitable provinces. The last years of Elizabeth were a Silver Age of profits, with no plague for over half a decade. There was a new production every two weeks, so there was always something to see: this year's novelties joined last year's big hits and, increasingly, an acknowledged masterpiece to be revived from the repertory of Elizabethan golden oldies. Shakespeare's works never left the repertory of the King's Men, right up to the closing of the theatres by Parliament during the Civil War.

The leading players of the King's Men were also co-owners of two theatres: the Globe and Blackfriars. Although this was

Woman's jacket,
c. 1600-25
Embroidered linen
with silk thread,
L (neck to hem)
66.5 cm
Victoria and Albert
Museum, London

unusual all companies had other assets, above all their plays, which were owned by the companies not the authors, and also the props and costumes.

The latter in particular were a huge investment. A good play and a good costume could easily cost the same. In 1603 Thomas Heywood was paid £6 for *A Woman Killed With Kindness*, while the heroine's black velvet dress cost £6 13s. The elaborate costumes for *Cardinal Wolsey* at the Fortune Theatre in 1601 cost the Admiral's Men £37 – the four contributing authors had to split £9 17s.6d. between them. Star-part costumes were expensive because they were originals: authentic aristocratic clothing, often bought from servants who inherited them as bequests from their noble masters and mistresses – which was the point of the bequest, since they were not legally allowed to wear such clothes. Costumes needed to earn their cost. Perhaps the most famous stage direction in history is in *The Winter's Tale*: 'Exit, pursued by a bear' (3.3.61). The King's Men had acquired a bear costume made for a royal masque and created a bear-centric season of three plays in which to use it.

There were other expenses, including payments to the court Master of Revels to license the performance of a new play and payments to license the playhouse itself. However, there were privately sponsored performances to bolster income. We know of

Possibly Lucy
Russell, Countess
of Bedford, by
unknown artist,
c. 1603
Oil on canvas,
H 191.4 cm,
W 113.8 cm
National Portrait
Gallery, London

two Shakespearean comedies, *The Comedy of Errors* and *Twelfth Night*, performed privately at the Inns of Court. Far more important were royal subsidies in the shape of command performances at court, usually several times during the Christmas season and around Shrovetide. Usually Elizabeth seems to have paid about £10 to Shakespeare's company for each of its Christmas performances, generally between three and six in number. Under James I court performances grew in importance and number, as plague outbreaks in London cut into the performing year. The first Christmas season of the new reign saw the King's Men alone earn £80 for giving six plays at Hampton Court, a larger sum than ever before, but this was against a backdrop of raging plague that devastated regular profits. The king gave them another £30 not to perform at this plague-racked time, presumably to restrain the gathering of crowds.

A full house at the Globe meant up to 3,000 heads, though a capacity crowd, when they really packed people in, might have been rare. Performance was continuous, with no intervals. Still, refreshment was constantly available, as a Swiss visitor, who saw *Julius Caesar* in 1599 at the newly-opened Globe, described: 'during the performance food and drink are carried around the audience, so that for what one cares to pay one may also have refreshment'. Bottle ales were available, as many references attest; reputedly, bottle ale was used to douse a man's burning breeches when the Globe burned down in 1613 during a performance of *Henry VIII*. Apples and nuts were among the favoured snacks and were sometimes used as missiles. Oysters, a pre-packed savoury, were consumed in large numbers and sweetmeats like gingerbread and sugar candy were available. 'An I had but one penny in the world, thou shouldst have it to buy gingerbread', Costard says in *Love's Labour's Lost* (5.1.49–50).

Noise, smells and little if any toilet provision were all part of the experience. One is also tempted to include the effects of weather, but seventy-five years of open-air performance at the start of the Little Ice Age has left few complaints about the rain or the cold. Bad light was a problem and John Webster blamed the lack of initial success of *The White Devil* in 1612 on 'so dull a time of winter'. Pickpockets and thieves were unsurprisingly present and an unwary visitor hosted by the Earl of Essex was once relieved of the huge sum of 300 crowns at a performance of Jonson's *Every Man in his Humour* at the Curtain Theatre in 1599. The more select and expensive indoor stages might spare their audiences some of this less refined company. 'A man shall not be choakte/ With the stench of Garlicke, nor be pasted/ To the barmy jacket of a Beer-Brewer', John Marston wrote in *Antonio's Revenge*, a play which, like *Hamlet*, featured a lot of theatrical in-jokes and audience-teasing comment.

Overall, the great open-air theatres for which Shakespeare wrote were cheap, popular and accessible. All human life was present on the stage, but it was also present in the audience, the monster that, in the words of child-star turned playwright, Nathan Field, 'clapt his thousand hands'. And, of course, was prepared to spend its money again.

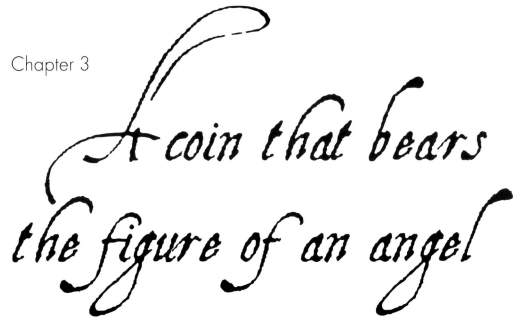

Chapter 3

A coin that bears the figure of an angel

English names and distant places

Prithee, peace.– Pay her the debt you owe her, and unpay
the villainy you have done her: the one you may do with
sterling money, and the other with current repentance.
(Henry IV Part 2, 2.1.84-6)

Sterling money was part of the medieval world of the
history plays, part of Shakespeare's own world and
is still part of our world today. References to the coins

and money of his daily life abound in the plays, even though none of these are in fact set in that contemporary world. His only plays set in England are histories and the reign of Henry VIII was as late as he would go. Instead the coins of English daily business circulate beneath the walls of Troy, in the markets of ancient Ephesus and republican Rome, in a wood near Athens and a castle at Elsinore, in Verona, Venice and Vienna. They are perhaps one way of making the past and the distant present and immediate; they also provide a shorthand way to indicate value and cost, wealth and poverty, charity and avarice, whatever notional setting his characters inhabit. Even when a desire for local colour or feeling of authenticity comes to the fore, Shakespeare still uses terms that are likely to be familiar to his audiences, from court to country inn-yard. Obscurity was not something he was seeking. If money is on stage, whether literally or metaphorically, then clarity is required for the point to get across, for the message to be heard.

Shakespeare's immediate, perhaps instinctive, preference was to use the money he and his audience both knew best, the currency of Elizabethan and Jacobean England.

Group of the kings of England Richard II, Henry IV, Henry V and Henry VI, by Hendrik Goltzius, 1584
Engraving on paper, H 14.6 cm, W 38.1 cm
British Museum, London

Such references overflow in the history plays. Shakespeare had some awareness that money was different in England's past, but the only obvious result of this was his use of the gold noble, worth 6s.8d. (a third of a pound and half a mark) and the principle high-value coin from 1351 to 1464. His historical sources, the Tudor chroniclers such as Hall and Holinshed, contained many a reference to this coin. The great quarrel between Bolingbroke and Mowbray that sets in motion the action of *Richard II* includes an accusation of the misuse of 8,000 nobles (1.1.88). Elsewhere one noble is a generous tip or payment at a lower level of society.

It is what the Shepherd, father of Joan la Pucelle (Joan of Arc),
gave the priest at his wedding, which he recalls as she is carried
stake-wards (*Henry VI Part 1*, 5.4.23) and the offer of a noble
calms the quarrel between Bardolph and Pistol in *Henry V*
(2.1.80-7). Like several English coin names, it offered itself up for
punning, as in the bitter wit of Richard of Gloucester:

> Myself disgraced, and the nobility
> Held in contempt, while great promotions
> Are daily given to ennoble those
> That scarce some two days since were worth a noble.

(*Richard III*, 1.3.78-81)

Yet the most common gold coin mentioned in the eight Wars of the
Roses plays is, anachronistically, the crown, the coin of 5-shillings.
This was only introduced in 1526 and was the standard gold coin
of Shakespeare's own day. Stores of crowns, purses of crowns, a
glove full of crowns promised by Henry V – they are everywhere.

The crown's rival was the angel, originally the replacement
for the noble as the coin of 6s.8d., but in Shakespeare's day worth
10 shillings. It was the commonest of a small number of coins
that preserved the virtually pure gold standard of the medieval
period, instead of the 22 carat 'crown gold'. By the 1590s it was
beginning to lose its place in regular currency, but it long retained
both a literary and a ceremonial life.

The angel's name derived from its design depicting the Archangel Michael defeating a dragon, a scene from the biblical Book of Revelation. This image, and its fine standards, gave the coin a special resonance. It was a prime vehicle for monetary jokes and in *King John* there are several, most notably in the mouth of the king himself (3.2.17–20):

Cousin, away for England! Haste before,
And ere our coming see thou shake the bags
Of hoarding abbots: imprisoned angels
Set at liberty

This is, of course, deeply unhistorical, as there was no gold coinage in thirteenth-century England, let alone angels. Similar angelic wordplay is found in *The Merry Wives* and *Henry IV Part 2*.

Yet the angel had more to offer Shakespeare than a quick clergy-baiting joke. He employed it in two more extended contexts. In the casket scenes in the *Merchant of Venice* (2.7), three suitors vying for the hand of Portia face a trial set by her deceased father, a choice between three caskets of gold, silver and lead. In classic fairy-tale manner, the poorest and youngest candidate wins by choosing lead, while the Prince of Arragon fails on silver, 'thou silver treasure-house', that turns out to be 'silvered o'er' – a plated counterfeit (2.9.33 and 69). A Spanish prince could hardly avoid choosing the metal on which his empire rested, thanks to the mines of Mexico and Peru. Similarly, the Prince of Morocco could hardly do otherwise than pick the gold that would be African in origin. In making his selection, he references the English angel in lyrical terms:

Or shall I think in silver she's immured,
Being ten times undervalued to trièd gold?
O sinful thought! Never so rich a gem
Was set in worse than gold! They have in England
A coin that bears the figure of an angel
Stamped in gold, but that's insculped upon,
But here an angel in a golden bed
Lies all within. Deliver me the key:
Here do I choose, and thrive I as I may!
(*The Merchant of Venice*, 2.7.52-60)

Shakespeare here turns a familiar coin into an exotic one, giving a sense of wonder to a standard item. Yet the angel already had this extra dimension. Increasingly its main role was in the ceremony of Touching for the King's Evil, in which the English monarch demonstrated his or her God-given healing power to cure the disease scrofula. Shakespeare would have had many opportunities to witness this ceremony at court, in which a pierced angel was placed around the neck of the sufferer. He described it in *Macbeth*, transposed to the remote Old English past of the saintly Edward the Confessor:

Angel of King James I pierced for use in the ceremony for Touching for the King's Evil, 1606-7
Gold, Diam. 2.9 cm
British Museum, London

'Tis called the evil:
A most miraculous work in this good king,
Which often, since my here-remain in England,
I have seen him do. How he solicits heaven
Himself best knows: but strangely-visited people,
All swoll'n and ulcerous, pitiful to the eye,
The mere despair of surgery, he cures,
Hanging a golden stamp about their necks,
Put on with holy prayers: and 'tis spoken,
To the succeeding royalty he leaves
The healing benediction. With this strange virtue
He hath a heavenly gift of prophecy,
And sundry blessings hang about his throne
That speak him full of grace.

(4.3.163-76)

Gold was always shorthand for monetary wealth, regardless of its actual nature. In Shakespeare's time Spanish wealth was often described in terms of gold, although it was the vast silver supplies of the New World that supported its empire. It was this silver that in reality made Shakespeare's world increasingly a monetary Silver Age, rather than a Golden.

Still alive in the memory was a poor silver coinage, the debased money of the mid-Tudor period. The removal of this, and her restoration of good money in 1560-1, was one of Elizabeth's early triumphs. Testern, tester or testril (from the word testoon), were terms used for the sorry debased shillings, usable for a while at a discounted rate, hence the air of contempt when characters use these coins. In *The Two Gentlemen of Verona* (1.1.123-8), the servant Speed is outraged by a testern tip: 'To testify your bounty, I thank you, you have testerned me; in requital whereof, henceforth carry your letters yourself'. To tip with a tester, as Falstaff and Sir Andrew Aguecheek also do, marks the cheapskate (*Henry IV Part 2*, 3.2.201; *Twelfth Night*, 2.3.22). Although long gone as a coin, it still had literary life in other playwrights' work as late as 1625. ('Wipe thy bum with testones' in *Eastward Ho!* in 1605 is perhaps the most pungent reference.)

England was now a land of good silver money, of the ancient sterling standard, famous and internationally trusted since the twelfth century. 'An if my word be sterling yet in England', is how the newly deposed Richard II musters any remaining authority he has (*Richard II*, 4.1.259). The larger silver coins, the half-groat of twopence, the threepence, the fourpenny groat, the sixpence and the 12-penny shilling, represented mid-range coins, between small change and gold – perhaps the equivalent of paper money in modern terms. The grand and powerful might disdain to deal with such sums: Coriolanus reports how his fearsome mother Volumnia is scornful of the world of daily shopping: 'things created/ To buy and sell with groats' (*Coriolanus*, 3.2.10 – 11); Prince Hal comments airily 'A trifle, some eight-penny matter' (*Henry IV Part 1*, 3.3.75). Yet sixpence a day is the fortune the missing Bottom might have earned, according to Flute, in *A Midsummer Night's Dream* (4.2.12 – 15):

Oh sweet bully Bottom! Thus hath he lost sixpence a day during his life; he could not have scaped sixpence a day. An the Duke had not given him sixpence a day for playing Pyramus, I'll be hanged. He would have deserved it. Sixpence a day in Pyramus, or nothing.

Scenes involving Falstaff's circle are particularly rich in English coin references – though notionally in the past, they are for all intents and purposes contemporary low-life and suburban scenes. Purse contents are listed. In *Henry IV Part 2* (1.2.162)

Base silver testoon of King Edward VI, 1549
Base silver, Diam. 2.9 cm
British Museum, London

Falstaff himself has seven groats and two pence (so 2s.6d. in total). In *The Merry Wives of Windsor* (1.1.108–110), Slender described the contents of his stolen purse: 'seven groats in mill-sixpences, and two Edward shovel-boards that cost me two shilling and two pence apiece of Yead Miller, by these gloves'. 'Mill-sixpences' were the machine-struck coins of Elizabeth made in the early 1560s, which were particularly treasured by contemporaries, and the 'Edward shovelboards' are wide shillings of Edward VI turned into pieces used in a popular game – the hapless Slender claims to have paid over double their face value for them. Falstaff also mentions 'shove-groat shillings' in *Henry IV, Part 2* (2.4.136). The mill-sixpences also seem to be overvalued (7 groats is 2s.4d. – not a sixpenny multiple), so none of his lost coins may have been actual currency – indeed there is evidence that sets of milled sixpences were used as high-quality reckoning counters.

Milled sixpence of
Queen Elizabeth I,
1562
Silver, Diam. 2.6 cm
British Museum,
London

Another altered silver coin crops up in *Henry VIII* (2.3.43–5). When Anne Bullen denies any wish to be queen 'for all the riches under heaven', the Old Lady drily replies: ''Tis strange: a three-pence bowed would hire me,/ Old as I am, to queen it', knowingly referencing a coin bent as a lover's gift.

Low value coins always seem to slip into proverbial form – not worth a cent, a penny, or a sou. We might think Shakespeare would use the lowest-value unit of English currency in this way: the quarter-penny or farthing. Yet nothing in Shakespeare is ever only worth a farthing, because there were none. By the sixteenth century a farthing of silver was a tiny thing, impracticable both to mint and to use, while halfpennies were only borderline practicable. For nearly a century England coped without farthings, and yet a farthing was still a viable sum of money, nearer a pound than a penny in modern terms. An Elizabethan solution was to introduce coins worth three-halfpence and three-farthings, so

Shilling of King Edward VI, 1551-3, turned into a gaming piece
Silver, Diam. 3.1 cm
British Museum, London

Three farting piece
of Queen
Elizabeth I, 1574
Silver, Diam. 1.2 cm
British Museum,
London

payments could be given and change received without actual halfpennies and farthings. It was ingenious, but a bit cumbersome, and halfpennies at least were returned to the silver currency.

There was an extended range of low-value Elizabethan coins, therefore, that Shakespeare could use to indicate small gradations of cheapness, from three-halfpence, through penny, three-farthings and halfpenny. To cope with this procession of slightly differently-sized little coins, a rose was added behind the head of the queen on alternate denominations. This provoked a numismatic joke in *King John* (1.1.143–4), in the mouth of the Bastard of Faulconbridge:

... in mine ear I durst not stick a rose,

Lest men should say, 'Look, where three-farthings goes!'.

Baffling to a modern audience, but easy topical humour at the time.

In *Henry V* (3.2.34–5) Bardolph is mocked for stealing a lute case, carrying it twelve leagues and then selling it for the tiny sum of three-halfpence; in *Love's Labour's Lost* (3.1.99–102), the clown Costard is tipped with a tiny three-farthing piece and is distracted into ecstasies from the paltriness of the gift by the Latinate circumlocution of the giver:

... 'Remuneration' – O, that's the Latin word for three farthings. Three farthings – remuneration. 'What's the price of this inkle?' 'One penny.' 'No, I'll give you a remuneration.' Why, it carries it. 'Remuneration.' Why, it is a fairer name than French crown. I will never buy and sell out of this word.

The worth of the French crown is built into the joke: the audience knows it is over fifty times the value of a three-farthing piece. However, Costard later gets a tip of a shilling, this time as a guerdon, a frenchified term, and shifts his response accordingly (3.1.128–9):

Gardon. O sweet gardon! Better than remuneration, a'leven-pence-farthing better.

In the last years of Elizabeth's reign, the revived halfpenny remained the smallest native coin available to suggest low value: halfpenny loaves are mentioned in *Henry VI Part 2* (4.2.49) and halfpenny purses in *The Merry Wives of Windsor* (3.5.99) and *Love's Labour's Lost* (5.1.51) as the cheapest possible versions. Jokes depend on the halfpenny's status as impossibly tiny and, as a result, indistinguishable. In *Much Ado About Nothing*, Leonato describes Beatrice's loss of temper: 'O, she tore the letter into a thousand halfpence, railed at herself that she should be so immodest to write to one that she knew would flout her' (2.3.108–11). And Rosalind in *As You Like It* jokes: 'There were none principal. They were all like one another as half-pence are, every one fault seeming monstrous till his fellow fault came to match it' (3.2.266–7).

And yet, something smaller than a halfpenny was needed to indicate virtual worthlessness and familiar foreign coins were brought into play. The French denier was one resort: Christopher Sly and Falstaff each resolve to pay 'not a denier' of claims on them (*Taming of the Shrew*, Induction Scene 1.6 and *Henry IV Part 1*, 3.3.55), while the soon-to-be Richard III exclaims 'My dukedom to a beggarly denier!' (*Richard III*, 1.2.261), all in plays of the 1590s.

More often called into play, however, was the Flemish and Dutch coin-name duit, anglicized as doit. Doits were familiar contemporary coins, the small change of the new Dutch Republic, and it is 'doit' that is Shakespeare's default term for near worthless coin. It became the standard term he used for low-value coins in

the ancient world, in *Timon of Athens* (1.1.235), *Pericles* (4.2.53–4) and *Coriolanus* (4.4.15–21):

Dutch doit, 1605
Alloy, Diam. 2 cm
British Museum,
London

Friends now fast sworn,

[...]

Unseparable, shall within this hour,

On a dissension of a doit, break out

To bitterest enmity

Twice the doit is quoted as the price of the cheapest entertainment, when in a quarrel Antony threatens Cleopatra with her place in Caesar's triumph:

French Maiolica
plate showing the
triumph of Julius
Caesar, after Taddeo
Zuccaro, 1600-30
Ceramic,
Diam. 48.5 cm
British Museum,
London

Let him take thee,
And hoist thee up to the shouting plebeians.
Follow his chariot, like the greatest spot
Of all thy sex. Most monster-like, be shown
For poor'st diminutives, for dolts

(Antony and Cleopatra, 4.12.35-9).

The same comparison in another perspective is to be found in *The Tempest* (2.2.24–8), as Trinculo muses on the potential for profit in the monstrous Caliban, with a familiar satirical sideswipe at English popular taste and an opportunity for the actor to give a comedy sneer at his audience:

A strange fish! Were I in England now — as once I was — and had but this fish painted, not a holiday fool there but would give a piece of silver: there would this monster make a man: any strange beast there makes a man: when they will not give a doit to relieve a lame beggar, they will lay out ten to see a dead Indian.

1613 saw the production of Shakespeare's last work in the theatre, but it also saw King James I's authorization of an issue of farthings, the first since the 1520s; not silver from the royal mint but tokens in copper. In the last years of his life he would have held and used an actual farthing coin - England's long-overdue answer to the doit.

Chapter 4

My ducats, and my daughter!

Setting the foreign scene

Moneys is your suit.

What should I say to you? Should I not say,

'Hath a dog money? Is it possible

A cur should lend thee three thousand ducats?'

(*The Merchant of Venice,* 1.3.110–13)

hen Shakespeare used the term doit in his plays set in the ancient world, he understood that this was a compromise: a term widely known, although not really accurate. He had done something like this in

his first classically-set play, *The Comedy of Errors*. The plot is derived from a Roman author and the setting is the ancient Mediterranean world, the Greek cities of Syracuse in Sicily and Ephesus in western Turkey. A trade war between them provides the back-story and money is everywhere, fundamental to the plot, but somewhat incoherently referenced. Modern monetary names abound, both English and foreign, angels and ducats, giving a contemporary feel to the frenzied and farcical goings-on. More often, however, Shakespeare used a different tactic.

He knew perfectly well what an ancient coin looked like after all, especially Roman ones. They could be found in the English soil then, as they can now, and collectors were already hunting them. One of the young gentleman-scholars in *Love's Labour's Lost*, heckling the pageant of the Nine Worthies, compared one to 'The face of an old Roman coin, scarce seen' (5.2.629). Shakespeare's main source for ancient history, Thomas North's translation of the Greek author Plutarch's *Lives*, in its 1579 edition, used engravings of ancient coin images, if often fantasy ones, at the head of each biography – of Coriolanus, Brutus, Caesar and Antony.

Julius Caesar is full of ancient coin references, including Mark Antony's reading of Caesar's will: 'Here is the will, and under Caesar's seal. To every Roman citizen he gives, To every several man, seventy-five drachmas' (3.2.237–9). And the military-funding quarrel between Brutus and Cassius:

Page from Thomas North's translation of Plutarch's *Lives of the Noble Grecians and Romanes* showing a woodcut of a coin of Brutus, 1579 British Library, London

THE LIFE OF
Marcus Brutus.

A   *Arcus Brutus* came of that *Iunius Brutus*, for whome the auncient Romanes made his statue of brasse to be set vp in the Capitoll, with the
images of the kings, holding a naked sword in his hand: bicause he had
valliantly put downe the Tarqvines from their kingdom of Rome.
But that *Iunius Brutus* being of a fower stearne nature, not softned by
reason, being like vnto sword blades of too hard a temper: was so sub-
iect to his choller and malice he bare vnto the tyrannes, that for their
sakes he caused his owne sonnes to be executed. But this *Marcus Bru-*
tus in contrarie maner, whose life we presently wryte, hauing framed
his manners of life by the rules of vertue and studie of Philosophie, and hauing imployed his
B wit, which was gentle and constant, in attempting of great things: me thinkes he was rightly
made and framed vnto vertue. So that his verie enemies which wish him most hurt, bicause
of his conspiracy against *Iulius Cæsar* : if there were any noble attempt done in all this conspiracie, they referre it whollie vnto *Brutus*, and all the cruell and violent actes vnto *Cassius*, who
was *Brutus* familiar frend, but not so well geuen, and condicioned as he. His mother *Seruilia*,
it is thought came of the blood of *Seruilius Hala*, who, when *Spurius Melius* went about to
make him selfe king, and to bring it to passe had entised the common people to rebell : tooke
a dagger and hid it close vnder his arme, and went into the market place. When he was come
thither, he made as though he had somewhat to say vnto him, and pressed as neere him as he
could : wherefore *Melius* stowping downe with his head, to heare what he would say, *Brutus*
C stabbed him in with his dagger, and slue him. Thus muche all writers agree for his mother.
Now touching his father, some for the euil wil & malice they bare vnto *Brutus*, bicause of the
death of *Iulius Cæsar*, doe maintaine that he came not of *Iunius Brutus* that draue out the Tarqvines : for there were none left of his race, considering that his two sonnes were executed
for conspiracie with the Tarqvines : and that *Marcus Brutus* came of a meane house, the
which was raised to honor and office in the common wealth, but of late time. *Posidonius* the
Philosopher wryteth the contrarie, that *Iunius Brutus* in deede slue two of his sonnes which

The parétage of Brutus.

Brutus ma-ners.

Seruilia M. Brutus mo-ther.

Brutus paren-tage by his father.

I did send to you

For certain sums of gold, which you denied me,

For I can raise no money by vile means:

By heaven, I had rather coin my heart

And drop my blood for drachmas, than to wring

From the hard hands of peasants their vile trash

By any indirection. I did send

To you for gold to pay my legions,

Which you denied me

(*Julius Caesar*, 4.3.133 – 41)

Shakespeare does not use the denarius, as a Latin writer would, but the Greek equivalent, the drachma. Here Shakespeare reflects his ultimate source, Plutarch, whose coin references were simply taken over by his sixteenth-century translators. However, this also meant that at least some of the audience for this play also knew the term.

In *Timon of Athens* the dominant monetary term is the talent: not really a coin name, but a measurement of weight and value. It is best known nowadays, and probably then also, from the Bible, so Shakespeare again is utilizing a term with some familiarity. The biblical talent was a very heavy standard. In ancient Athens, the talent was lighter, but still substantial: 26 kg, or 57 lb of silver. It was equivalent to 6,000 Athenian drachmas and would pay the crew of a warship for a month. Timon is a partnership play, the work of Shakespeare and Thomas Middleton (1570? – 1627),

each writing different acts, and one of the ways of differentiating them is the usage of 'talent', with Shakespeare seemingly recognizing its high value, and keeping totals small – a realistic three or five talents. References to fifty and, on one occasion, to a thousand talents are impossibly huge sums and suggest a different, and inaccurate, understanding of the term – or, alternatively, a deliberately flagrant raising of the stakes.

In foreign-set plays with a more contemporary feel, Shakespeare uses two foreign coins above all others, ones that are both familiar enough to give his audience a sense of the values involved, while also providing a bit of local colour. Ducats are everywhere, more than fifty references across ten plays. The ducat was in origin the defining gold coin of Venice, but the term also meant any coin of the same standard and it was widely used and familiar. Still, its prime locale was Italy and most Shakespearean references are in Italian-set plays. In the Paduan setting of *The Taming of the Shrew*, one of Bianca's suitors offers a dower of property in Pisa and 2,000 ducats a year (2.1.368– 71), while in Verona Romeo pays 40 ducats for a dram of poison (*Romeo and Juliet*, 5). In *The Two Gentlemen of Verona*, Speed pointedly notes the lack of a ducat tip (1.1.121). Both Padua and Verona were part of Venice's Italian territories. A hefty 1,000-ducat bribe propels the

Venetian ducat of
Marino Grimani,
Doge of Venice,
1595-1605
Gold, Diam. 2 cm
British Museum,
London

plot of the Sicilian-set *Much Ado About Nothing*, while in *Twelfth Night*, in Italianate Illyria, Sir Andrew Aguecheek has an excellent income of 3,000 ducats a year (1.3.17).

In the coin's original home Antonio, the Merchant of Venice himself, fatefully offers the surety of a pound of flesh for a loan of 3,000 ducats from Shylock. This 3,000 ducat debt bounces through the plot, offered, refused, lamented and transferred. Elsewhere in this money-drenched play, Shylock's daughter Jessica is prodigal with her father's ducats, raiding his store for her elopement ('I will make fast the doors, and gild myself/ With some more ducats, and be with you straight', *Merchant of Venice*, 2.6.50). We hear Shylock's hysterical reaction, in mocking report:

Salanio:

> I never heard a passion so confused...
> As the dog Jew did utter in the streets:
> My daughter! Oh my ducats! Oh, my daughter!
> Fled with a Christian! Oh, my Christian ducats!
> Justice! The Law! My ducats, and my daughter!
> A sealed bag, two sealed bags of ducats,
> Of double ducats, stolen from me by my daughter!...

Salarino:

> Why all the boys in Venice follow him,
> Crying his stones, his daughter and his ducats!

The most excellent

Historie of the Merchant
of Venice.

VVith the extreame crueltie of *Shylocke* the Iewe
towards the fayd Merchant, in cutting a iuſt pound
of his fleſh : and the obtayning of *Portia*
by the choyſe of three
cheſts.

As it hath beene diuers times acted by the Lord
Chamberlaine his Seruants.

Written by William Shakeſpeare.

AT LONDON,
Printed by *I. R.* for Thomas Heyes,
and are to be ſold in Paules Church-yard, at the
ſigne of the Greene Dragon.
1600.

When Shylock himself is onstage and aghast at Jessica's prodigality, the audience is meant to know what a ducat represents – maybe £50 or more in our terms – and will recognize the genuine extravagance.

Tubal:

> Your daughter spent in Genoa, as I hear, in one night fourscore ducats.

Shylock:

> Thou stickest a dagger in me. I shall never see my gold again; fourscore ducats at a sitting! Fourscore ducats!

While Antonio offers his beloved friend Bassanio his purse and his person and starts the plot, Shylock laments his ducats and his daughter and prepares his vengeance: money does make the Venetian world go round.

Ducats feature in *Hamlet*'s Denmark ('How now? A rat? Dead, for a ducat, dead!', 3.4.27) and in the Viennese-set *Measure For Measure*, both places with their own versions of the ducat. Most unexpected is the 10,000-ducat bet on the fidelity of Innogen in the ancient British world of *Cymbeline* (1.4.92–3) – admittedly the setting for the bet is Rome, but with a Frenchman, Dutchman and Spaniard in attendance, historical fidelity is barely a factor.

Referenced in seven plays is the French crown, the écu à la couronne, the most familiar foreign gold coin in Tudor England. Certainly Bottom's rhapsody on yellow in *A Midsummer Night's Dream* (1.2.68–70) seemed to expect audience recognition:

I will discharge it in either your straw-colour beard, your orange-tawny beard, your purple-in-grain beard, or your French-crown-coloured beard, your perfect yellow.

It is no surprise to find French crowns in *Henry IV Part 2* (3.2.162) and *Henry V* (4.1.181), here also under its French name of écu (4.4.37), since an invasion of France is depicted. In *Henry VI Part 2*, the low-born rebel Jack Cade jeers 'Go to, sirrah, tell the king from me, that for his father's sake, Henry the Fifth, in whose time boys went to span-counter for French crowns, I am content he shall reign: but I'll be Protector over him' (4.2.123–5). French crowns are also casually mentioned in the French-set plays *Love's Labour's Lost* (3.1.102) and *All's Well That Ends Well* (2.2.14).

During James I's reign a new foreign coin makes its appearance in the plays, another useful for word-play: the dollar. It features in a little cluster of early Jacobean works in 1603-6 (*King Lear*, *Macbeth* and *Measure For Measure*) and is given a further mention in *The Tempest* in 1611. The anglicized version of the German thaler, it referred generally to a large silver coin

Crown (écu) of King
Henry III of France,
1574-89
Gold, Diam. 2.4 cm
British Museum,
London

and could mean anything from actual thalers to Spanish pieces of eight. It was a denomination in James's Scottish coinage and the one straightforward usage of the term is set in Scotland, when a lord reports the terms given to a defeated invader (*Macbeth*, 1.2.66-8):

Nor would we deign him burial of his men
Till he disbursèd at Saint Colme's inch
Ten thousand dollars to our general use

In the other plays, the usage seems to derive from the similarity of dollar and dolour – grief. This gave it a literary usefulness that overcame any implausible anachronism in *King Lear* (2.2.225-32), as the Fool mordantly jokes:

Fathers that wear rags
Do make their children blind,
But fathers that bear bags
Shall see their children kind.
Fortune, that arrant whore,
Ne'er turns the key to th'poor.
But, for all this, thou shalt have as many dolours for thy
daughters as thou canst
tell in a year.

The same sort of wordplay occurs in *The Tempest* (2.1.17–18).

In contrast to ducats, French crowns, doits and dollars, there are some foreign coins that appear only in one play: crusado, guilder, chequin and quart d'ecu are among these. On the assumption that Shakespeare did not use coin names to confuse or puzzle, we need to account for these singleton appearances.

The guilder makes an early debut in *The Comedy of Errors*, among the prodigal welter of coin names that characterize that play. Guilder is an anglicization of *gulden*, the principal gold coin of Germany and the Low Countries. The duke of Ephesus sets the story going by condemning to death the plot's patriarch Egeon, father of the Antipholus twins, in reaction to the hanging of some Ephesian merchants, 'wanting guilders to redeem their lives' (1.1.8). Later a generic Second Merchant demands repayment of debts from the wrong increasingly-bewildered Antipholus twin: 'I am bound/ To Persia and want guilders for my voyage' (4.1.3–4). This merchant is as much Dutch as Ephesian, preparing to sail east, as so many Dutch merchants did. For a flicker of a moment, we are in the Amsterdam headquarters of the Dutch East India Company, not ancient Anatolia.

A similar reference is to be found in the other play that spans the ancient eastern Mediterranean, *Pericles, Prince of Tyre*. On the island of Lesbos, the rueful brothel-owner Pander comments 'Three or four thousand chequins were as pretty a proportion to live quietly' (4.2.27–8). The word chequin, or sequin, derived from *zecchino*, the ducat's name in Venice itself. The term was used in English

Crusado of King
Joao III of Portugal,
1521-57
Gold, Diam. 2 cm
British Museum,
London

for ducat-derived coins of Turkey and was an entirely apposite coin for an eastern Mediterranean locale in Shakespeare's day, if not the notional time of Prince Pericles. A contemporary text gives the current value of the chequin as 7s.2d., so Pandar's claim for the sum is accurate, as 3,000 chequins was a little over £1,000, over double the annual profits of the King's Men.

All's Well That Ends Well is set in a vaguely medieval France and two of its characters, the courtiers Parolles (4.3.203) and Lafew (5.2.23) use the term quart d'écu (or cardecue) in contexts that suggest a mid-range sum – Lafew gives one as a tip. This is fair enough, as the silver quart d'écu of contemporary France was worth something between a shilling and a half-crown in English terms. The coin was common enough in early seventeenth-century England for counterfeit versions to be a problem and Fletcher and Massinger mention it in *The Elder Brother* (c. 1625), so it is a case of Shakespeare using a familiar coin to provide appropriate local colour.

Shakespeare's usage of the coin-name crusado in *Othello* (3.4.20) provides his only clear reference to Portuguese coins. As it occurs in a play set firmly in the Venetian world of Venice itself and its colony of Cyprus, it is a surprise to find it present, almost as surprising as the total absence of the ducats that suffuse *The Merchant of Venice*. The reference occurs as Desdemona pushes away any thought of Othello being jealous:

Believe me, I had rather have lost my purse
Full of crusadoes: and but my noble Moor
Is true of mind and made of no such baseness
As jealous creatures are

(*Othello*, 3.4.19-22)

The gold crusado was another ducat-based coin, earning its name from its prominent cross design. Portuguese gold coinage flourished because of Portugal's Atlantic trade with the gold coast of Africa. Since the relations of Europe and Africa provide crucial underpinning to *Othello*, it is tempting to see the African connection lying behind this unexpected coin. Yet, there is another dimension to the play, the war against the Turks. The usual English meaning of crusado, encountered far more often than the coin in contemporary literature, was crusade.

Chapter 5

Now do I play the touch

Metaphors of money

Albeit I will confess thy father's wealth
Was the first motive that I wooed thee, Anne,
Yet, wooing thee, I found thee of more value
Than stamps in gold or sums in sealèd bags.
And 'tis the very riches of thyself
That now I aim at.

(*The Merry Wives of Windsor*, 3.4.14 – 19)

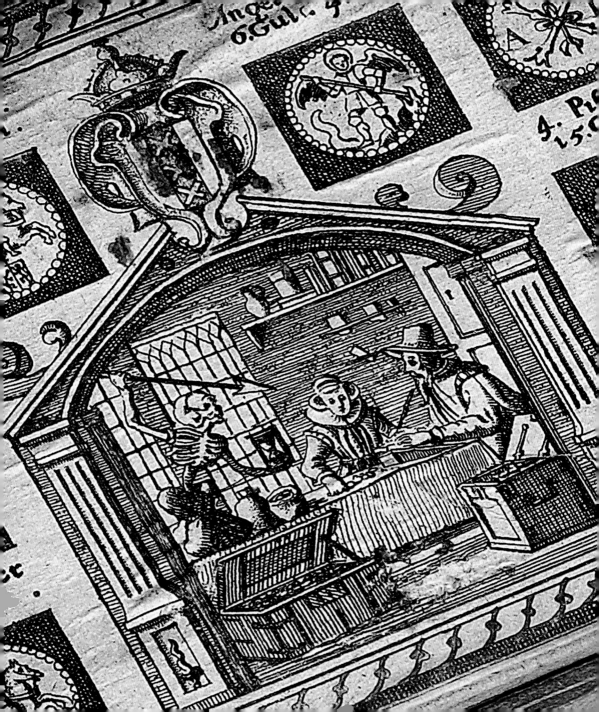

*H*ere the young gentleman Fenton comes clean about what first attracted him to heiress Anne Page. But he shifts her riches from her purse to her person: she is rich in metaphorical terms, even if the 'seven hundred pounds of moneys, and gold

and silver' to come from her grandsire (1.1.32–3) make for substantial icing on the cake.

The way coinage was treated in currency in early modern England created an assemblage of variously useful shorthand symbols and similes, providing a way of concisely expressing aspects of the human condition, and it was an option that the dramatists of the time turned to readily.

All English money was gold or silver, and precious-metal coins need looking after, especially gold ones. The value of the coin had a direct relationship to it being of the right fineness and weight. This is what the stamp of authority, the image on a coin, guaranteed and purpose-made equipment – coin weights and balances – assisted in this. People therefore were on the watch for under-value coins – either

☞
Dutch hand balance and coin-weights, by Guillaum de Neve, 1600–54
Wood and brass, box L 15 cm, W 9 cm, balance H 15 cm, W 11 cm
British Museum, London

reduced by clipping or wear, or else straightforward counterfeits. Gold coins were examined most closely, while the lesser silver denominations more readily passed without much scrutiny: much as a £50 note and a £1 coin will receive different levels of retailer attention today. In Shakespeare's plays there are many allusions to the ingrained habit of checking and testing money, but often they are not actually about money. They are about people. When Falstaff reproaches Prince Hal, 'Never call a true piece of gold a counterfeit: thou art essentially made, without seeming so' (*Henry IV Part 1*, 2.4.360-1), he is talking about himself.

In *Cymbeline*, Posthumus Leonatus prays for the survival of his wife Innogen, using the image of humanity as the coinage of the gods:

For Innogen's dear life take mine, and though
'Tis not so dear, yet 'tis a life; you coined it.
'Tween man and man they weigh not every stamp:
Though light, take pieces for the figure's sake.
You rather mine, being yours: and so, great powers,
If you will take this audit, take this life,
And cancel these cold bonds.
(5.4.125-31)

Posthumus asks for their lives to be reckoned by tale - by count - as Innogen's life is more worthy than his, a coin of better weight.

Anyone handling gold coins would readily examine them closely, weigh them, and test them with a needle or touchstone if suspicious – they could be highly sensitive to differences in the weight and colour of metals. Several casual comments or asides in the plays acknowledge this basic habit. When in *Henry IV Part 2* (1.2.118), the Chief Justice rebukes Falstaff as Prince Hal's 'evil angel', the latter turns it into one of his many coinage jokes: 'Not so, my lord, your ill angel is light: but I hope that he that looks

The Covetous Man, by David Teniers the Younger, *c.* 1648
Oil on canvas, H 62.5 cm, W 85 cm
National Gallery, London

upon me will take me without weighing' (1.2.118–20). In *All's Well That Ends Well*, a letter asks about someone: 'whether he thinks it were not possible, with well-weighing sums of gold, to corrupt him to a revolt' (4.3.129–30) and *Pericles* references 'gold, that's by the touchstone tried' (2.2.38).

There is, of course, a living Touchstone in Shakespeare, in *As You Like It*, a court fool, who tests the judgment and intelligence of those about him. This may be an in-joke. Robert Armin, the actor who probably played the part, began as a goldsmith and knew his way around a touchstone.

Falstaff's point about the importance of telling true gold from counterfeit is based on how essential that was in practice, but it also fed into common anxieties about legitimacy, truth and authenticity. The terminology of testing quality therefore was easily transferred to the human sphere, the testing of honesty and loyalty. Richard III mutters: 'Ah, Buckingham, now do I play the touch,/ To try if thou be current gold' (*Richard III*, 4.2.9–10). In *Measure for Measure*, Angelo fatefully offers himself up for testing before accepting office (1.1.50–3):

Now, good my lord,
Let there be some more test made of my mettle,
Before so noble and so great a figure
Be stamped upon it

THE
History of the two Maids of More-clacke,

VVith the life and simple maner of IOHN
in the Hospitall.

Played by the Children of the Kings
Maiesties Reuels.

VVritten by ROBERT ARMIN, seruant to the Kings
most excellent Maiestie.

LONDON,
Printed by *N.O.* for *Thomas Archer*, and is to be sold at his
shop in Popes-head Pallace, 1 6 0 9.

All this testing and trying points to the prevalence of the untrue and counterfeit, as is, of course, intended. Coinage was the prerogative of kings. It is a well-aimed blow when, in *King John*, Constance rebukes the King of France:

You have beguiled me with a counterfeit
Resembling majesty, which, being touched and tried,
Proves valueless
(3.1.25-7)

Any counterfeit should, of course, be rejected, as Cardinal Campeius says, in stiffening the resolve of Queen Katherine in *Henry VIII* (3.1.182-5):

... you wrong your virtues
With these weak women's fears. A noble spirit,
As yours was put into you, ever casts
Such doubts as false coin from it.

The Cardinal language was doubly misogynistic, as it was then a commonplace that women were more likely to be fooled by counterfeit coin. A character in Thomas Middleton's *Revenger's Tragedy* notes: 'Women are apt you know to take false money' (1.1.103).

Gilded twopence
(half-groat) of
Queen Elizabeth I,
1560-1
Silver, Diam. 1.8 cm
British Museum,
London

A particular form of fake noted by Shakespeare and others was the turning of a genuine silver coin into a fake gold one, specifically gilding the twopence, which was similar in size and design to the gold half-crown. Falstaff uses 'gilt two-pences' to make a point in *Henry IV Part 2* (4.1.396) and in *Troilus and Cressida* Thersites, who 'coins slanders like a mint' (1.3.194), insults Patroclus as a 'gilt counterfeit'(2.3.16), perhaps this same topical form of forgery.

Half-crown of
Queen Elizabeth I,
1560-1
Gold, Diam. 1.8 cm
British Museum,
London

The technology of coin-making, stamping a piece of metal between two dies, was straightforward and well-understood. Two different objects come together to produce a third that reproduces elements of both. It thus offered a ready metaphor for human reproduction, all the more so because of the difference between genuine coins, legitimately made from a legally-authorized union of official instruments, and counterfeit coins, illegal, illicit and illegitimate. Richard of Gloucester, the ultimate monster both physically and morally, is 'rudely stamped' – a mis-struck coin (*Richard III*, 1.1.16). Those having extra-marital sex, according to Angelo in *Measure for Measure*, 'do coin heaven's image/ In stamps that are forbid' (2.4.45–6), going on to equate murder with siring a bastard, through an analogy with the capital crime of counterfeiting:

'tis all as easy
Falsely to take away a life true made
As to put mettle in restrainèd means
To make a false one.
(2.4.46–9).

In *Edward III*, which Shakespeare may have co-written, the Countess of Salisbury wards off the amorous king in similar terms:

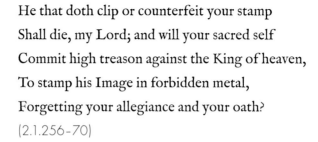

He that doth clip or counterfeit your stamp

Shall die, my Lord; and will your sacred self

Commit high treason against the King of heaven,

To stamp his Image in forbidden metal,

Forgetting your allegiance and your oath?

(2.1.256-70)

Siring a bastard is counterfeiting God's coin, and a king, above all, should respect coinage. In *Cymbeline*, Posthumus, fooled into believing his wife Innogen unfaithful, pushes the idea of bastard as counterfeit to the limit:

Is there no way for men to be, but women

Must be half-workers? We are all bastards,

And that most venerable man, which I

Did call my father, was I know not where

When I was stamped. Some coiner with his tools

    Made me a counterfeit

     (2.4.194-9)

Along with stamping and coining, weighting and testing, comes accounting and reckoning. Accounting in the plays can take the form of Falstaff's straightforward comedy outlays: 'Item, A capon, 2s 2d. Item, Sauce, 4d. Item, Sack, two

81

Arithmetica from
*The Seven Liberal
Arts*, by George
Glover, 1625-35
Engraving on paper,
H 20.2 cm, W 13.5 cm
British Museum,
London

ARITHMETICA.

Thy depth ARITHMETICK there's none can knowe,
since from bare one, such Countles numbers growe
Wᵗʰ multiply'de, to Infinites it comes,
making base counters, stand for Goulden summes. 5

gallons, 5s 8d. Item, Anchovies and sack after supper, 2s.6d. Item, Bread, ob (i.e. halfpenny)' (*Henry IV Part 1*, 2.4.397–8). Prompting Prince Hal's exclamation: 'O, monstrous! But one halfpenny-worth of bread to this intolerable deal of sack?' (2.4.399–400). Then there is the parody accounting of Olivia's treatment of clichéd love poetry in *Twelfth Night* (1.5.179): 'item, two lips, indifferent red: item, two grey eyes, with lids to them...' Finally there is the grim reckoning of a human life, the ultimate calling to account, as summarized by the philosophical First Jailer in *Cymbeline*:

A heavy reckoning for you, sir. But the comfort is you shall be called to no more payments, fear no more tavern-bills, which are as often the sadness of parting as the procuring of mirth: you come in faint for want of meat, depart reeling with too much drink: sorry that you have paid too much and sorry that you are paid too much: purse and brain both empty: the brain the heavier for being too light, the purse too light, being drawn of heaviness. Of this contradiction you shall now be quit. O, the charity of a penny cord! It sums up thousands in a trice: you have no true debitor and creditor but it: of what's past, is, and to come, the discharge: your neck, sir, is pen, book and counters; so the acquittance follows.

(5.3.257–66)

Pen, book and counters are the tools of accounting, the counters being specially-made coin-like discs moved around on a checkerboard, much like using an abacus. A bag or cylinder of counters formed the pocket calculator of the time. In *The Winter's Tale* we observe country folk using this method, as the Clown puzzles over his errands:

I cannot do't without counters. Let me see, what am I to buy for our sheep-shearing feast? Three pound of sugar, five pound of currants, rice— what will this sister of mine do with rice?

(4.3.32–4)

German reckoning-counter showing a checkerboard being used for counting
Alloy, Diam. 2.8 cm
British Museum, London

Translated to the metaphorical level and remote in both time and social space Prince Troilus argues with Hector about the cost of keeping Helen at Troy:

Fie, fie, my brother!
Weigh you the worth and honour of a king
So great as our dread father in a scale
Of common ounces? Will you with counters sum
The past proportion of his infinite ...?

(*Troilus and Cressida*, 2.2.26–30).

Ordinary folk used base-metal counters, often called jettons nowadays, but the wealthy would use sets of silver ones, carried in silver containers.

Few, if any, of these monetary metaphors are peculiar to Shakespeare. Tropes of coining – false and true, sterling or base; of reckoning, weighing and testing; of trying and striking: these were well-used features of the dramatic and literary world he inhabited, as well as being part of the actual world around him, where currency and counterfeits operated
both literally and

Set of silver counters
by Simon Passe
showing the Stuart
royal family, 1600s
Silver box containing
twenty-nine silver
medals, each Diam.
2.6 cm
British Museum,
London

by analogy. The stakes were high where money was concerned. A government informer asserted that, among many subversive statements, Shakespeare's great predecessor Christopher Marlowe had claimed 'as good Right to Coine as the Queen of England', making money in the most literal sense. Money of precious metal had an absorbing physicality perhaps hard for us now to grasp – its form and fineness fundamental to its role. Bank money existed and paper transfers were well-established, but there is only one reference to 'bills for money by exchange' in all of Shakespeare's plays, from Florence, appropriately enough for this great centre of banking and bills of exchange (*Taming of the Shrew*, 3.4.94). Otherwise hard cash rules.

Epilogue

Repose, sweet gold

I began with the uncovering of a hoard of gold in one of Shakespeare's last plays, so perhaps it is appropriate to consider the deposition of a hoard of gold in one of his earliest. In *Titus Andronicus* (2.3.1-8), the Moor Aaron chats to the audience while burying his stolen treasure,

He that had wit would think that I had none,
To bury so much gold under a tree
And never after to inherit it.
Let him that thinks of me so abjectly
Know that this gold must coin a stratagem,
Which, cunningly effected, will beget
A very excellent piece of villainy:

M.r Henry Peacham author of the
compleate gentleman

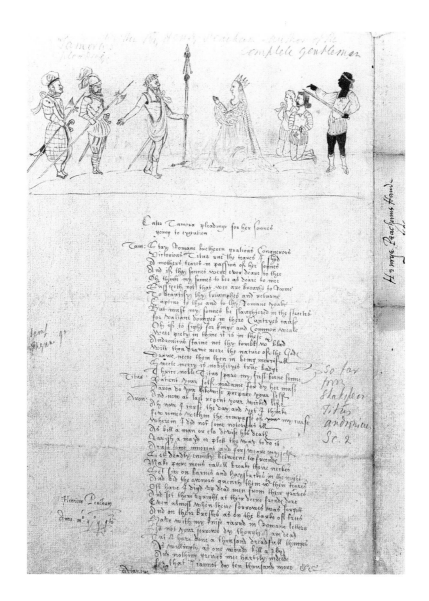

H.S mye. Peachams Hand

Enter Tamora pleadinge for her sonnes
goinge to execution

Tam: Stay Romane bretheren gratious Conquerors
Victorious Titus rue the teares I shed
A mothers teares in passion for her sonne
And if thy sonnes were ever deare to thee
Ohe thinke my sonnes to bee as deare to mee
Sufficeth not that wee are brought to Roome
To beautifye thy triumphes and returne
Captive to thee and to thy Romane yoake
But must my sonnes be slaughtered in the streetes
For valiant doeinges in their Cuntryes cause
Ohe if to fight for kinge and Common weale
Were piety in thyne it is in these
Andronicus staine not thy tombe w:th blood
Wilt thou drawe neere the nature of the Gods
Drawe neere them then in beinge mercifull
Sweete mercy is nobilityes true badge

Titus Thrice noble Titus spare my first borne sonne
Patient your self madame for by her most

Aron Reason doe you likewise and prepare your self
And now at last repent your heavie lott
Ah now I curse the day and yet I thinke
Few come within the compasse of my curse
Wherein I did not some notorious ill
As kill a man or els devise his death
Ravish a maide or plott the way to do it
Accuse some innocent and forsweare my self
Set deadly enmity betweene two freendes
Make poore mens cattell breake theire neckes
Set fire on barnes and haystackes in the night
And bid the owners quench them w:th theire teares
Oft have I digd vp dead men from theire graves
And set them vprighte at theire deere freendes doore
Even almost when theire sorrowes was forgott
And on their breastes as on the barke of trees
Have with my knife carved in Romane letters
Lett not your sorrowe dye though I am dead
Tut I have done a thousand dreadfull thinges
As willingly as one would kill a fly
And nothing greeves mee hartily indeede
But that I cannot doo ten thousand more

So far
from
Shakspeare
Titus
andronicus
Sc. 2

89

And so repose, sweet gold, for their unrest

[Hides the gold]

That have their alms out of the empress' chest.

Aaron chose a site under a tree, a landmark to indicate the spot should he need to return, something many of Shakespeare's contemporaries would have done in an age without secure banks. An unfortunate few would fail to return, to leave the hoards we find today. In early modern lore, Aaron's ghost might well have haunted the treasure site, as Horatio suggests to the Ghost of Hamlet's father:

Or if thou hast uphoarded in thy life

Extorted treasure in the womb of earth –

For which, they say, you spirits oft walk in death –

Speak of it: stay and speak!

(1.1.127-30)

The fairies, as well as the dead, hovered over treasure: 'This is fairy gold, boy, and 'twill prove so. Up with't, keep it close', says the Old Shepherd in *The Winter's Tale* (3.3.105), finding the baby Perdita and the riches left with her.

Money could hold and motivate characters beyond death or any prohibition. 'Bell, book and candle shall not drive me back,/ When gold and silver becks me to come on', the Bastard

of Faulconbridge jauntily remarks in *King John*, in defiance of excommunication (3.2.23–4).

Shakespeare, money and medals have an association that would long survive. There was no medal of Shakespeare during his life – of course not – but he has more than made up for that since. His medallic legacy took some time to get going. Dassier's medal of 1731 seems to be the first and numbers grew as the cult of Shakespeare flourished – the Stratford Jubilee medal of 1769, society medals, prize medals, commemoratives of his birth and death and medals to mark the publication of his works, like the subscription medal of 1803.

Shakespeare was one of the eclectic group of individuals used in place of the king's head on the 'medley halfpennies' of the late eighteenth century, unofficial small change circumventing the counterfeiting laws. He also appeared, unsurprisingly on the more legitimate tokens of Warwickshire and on local banknotes. He presided on the £20 note for many years, his hologram shimmers on credit cards, and lines from his plays feature on the 2012 commemorative coins.

We can be sure Shakespeare had a healthy regard for money; but did coins as such interest him? His many coin-references might suggest so. One of his colleagues certainly thought he would appreciate a fine gold coin. In May 1605 Augustine Philips died, a member of Shakespeare's company from its beginning. In his will he left sums of money to the hired

British Medal, designed by Conrad Heinrich Küchler, 1803
Gold, Diam. 4.8 cm
British Museum, London

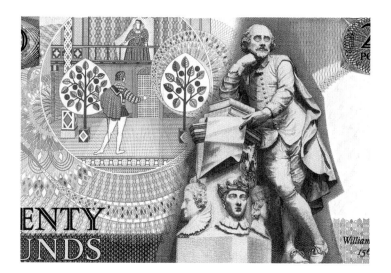

Detail of a £20 note
with a portrait of
Shakespeare, 1970
Banknote, L 14 cm,
W 8.5 cm
British Museum,
London

men of the troupe and his present and past apprentices. He began his bequests, however, somewhat differently. 'Item I geve and bequeathe to my ffellowe William Shakespeare a Thirty shillinges peece in gould.'

Shakespeare's gold piece is the first such bequest, to be followed by the same given to two other members of the King's Men. The coin given is a quite specific one, a 30-shilling sovereign of Elizabeth I, one of the few coins that, like the angel, still maintained the virtually pure medieval standard of fineness. We know that Queen Elizabeth would normally make gifts to entertainers who pleased her in angels or other fine gold 'for a gracious reward by her majesty's commandment'. It is possible that the coins of Philip's bequest originated in some specific sign of royal favour or enjoyment that Shakespeare would recognize. A character in Ben Jonson's play *The Alchemist* has another such fine-gold coin, a spur-ryal of James I ('I have a paper with a spur ryal in't'), kept as a pocket piece. Philip's bequest to Shakespeare is such a thing, a memento and a keepsake. Of course, we have no way of knowing if Shakespeare kept it to hand as a memorial of long fellowship, or if he simply added it to his savings or his ready cash.

It has been said that you could remove all references to coins from Shakespeare's plays, and it would make little difference. Yet there are many other subjects for which this might equally hold true. It is the combination of references that gives the density to the worlds Shakespeare delineates, worlds that are simultaneously distant and immediate. It is in the latter area that coin references come into their own, realizing the fabric of the plays' settings in remote historical time and distant geographic location by drawing on the experiences and knowledge of the audience. Words, not elaborate period detail, set the scene in Italy, France or the classical world and the names of coins are part of this, so long as the audience recognizes them. Similarly, their known value firms up awareness of what is at stake in the plots. Nowadays they seem obscure, sometimes a barrier to understanding. We need to understand these references to comprehend the language, the ideas, the jokes and the metaphors on the stage before us.

What is here?
Gold? Yellow, glittering, precious gold?

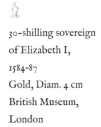

30-shilling sovereign of Elizabeth I, 1584-87
Gold, Diam. 4 cm
British Museum, London

Further reading

Melissa D. Aaron, *Global economies: a history of the theatre business, the Chamberlain's/ King's Men and their plays, 1599-1642* (Newark, 2005)

D.F. Allen and W.R. Dunstan, '"Crosses and crowns": a study of coinage in the Elizabethan dramatists', *British Numismatic Journal* 23 (1941), 287-99.

Neil Carson, *A Companion to Henslowe's Diary* (Cambridge, 1988)

J. Eric Engstrom, *Coins in Shakespeare: a numismatic guide* (Hanover, 1964)

Sandra K. Fischer, *Econolingua: glossary of coins and economic language in Renaissance drama* (Delaware, 1985)

Andrew Gurr, *Playgoing in Shakespeare's London* (3rd edition, Cambridge, 2004)

Rosalyn Lander Knutson, *Playing companies and commerce in Shakespeare's time* (Cambridge, 2001)

Theodore B. Leinwand, *Theatre, finance and society in early modern England* (Cambridge, 1999)

Linda Woodbridge (ed.), *Money and the age of Shakespeare: essays in new economic criticism* (New York, 2003)

Image credits

Except where otherwise stated, photographs are © The Trustees of the British Museum, courtesy of the Department of Photography and Imaging. British Museum registration numbers are listed below. Further information about the Museum and its collection can be found at britishmuseum.org

p. 2 By permission of the Governors of Stonyhurst College

pp. 10, 16 CM M.6903

pp. 12–13 © British Library Board

p. 15 PE WB.180 Bequeathed by Baron Ferdinand Anselm de Rothschild

p. 17 (above) CM 1844,0425.24

p. 17 (below) PD 1874,0613.2504

pp. 18–19 CM 1882,0507.1 Donated by Sir Augustus Wollaston Franks

p. 21 PD 1880,1113.5315

p. 23, 32 © Victoria and Albert Museum, London

pp. 24–5, 28 PD 1864,0611.434

p. 26 Utrecht, University Library

p. 33 © National Portrait Gallery, London

pp. 36, 43 CM 1954,1002.8 Bequeathed by Miss Helen Farquhar

p. 39 PD 1928,1212.43

p. 44 CM 1935,0401.1790 Bequeathed by Thomas Bryan Clarke-Thornhill

p. 46 CM 1946,1004.419

p. 47 CM 2011,4071.1

p. 48 CM 1915,0507.152

p. 51 CM 1870,0507.9932

p. 52 PE 2008,8003.1 Acquired with contribution from British Museum Friends

pp. 55, 59 CM 1862,1001.350

pp. 56–7 © British Library Board

p. 60 © British Library Board

pp. 62–3 CM 1935,0401.10599 Bequeathed by Thomas Bryan Clarke-Thornhill

p. 66 CM 1971,0606.7

pp. 69-71 CM W.3132

p. 73 The National Gallery, London

p. 75 By Permission of the Folger Shakespeare Library

p. 77 (above) CM 1935,0401.2324 Bequeathed by Thomas Bryan Clarke-Thornhill

p. 77 (below) CM 1915,0507.523

p. 78 Superstock

p. 80 CM H.38

p. 81 PD 1875,0410.174 Donated by James Hughes Anderdon

p. 82 PD 1870,0514.1142

pp. 84-5 CM J.0117

p. 86 CM M.6915

p. 89 © Marquess of Bath

p. 91 CM G3,IP.1026 Donated by King George IV

p. 92 CM CIB.7961 Donated by ifs School of Finance

p. 93 CM E.300

Acknowledgements

I am grateful for many things to the Keeper of Coins and Medals, Philip Attwood, my long-time colleague, but in this instance he read and commented on this text to its great advantage. Helen Wang similarly gave excellent advice and enthusiastic encouragement. Dora Thornton of the Department of Prehistory and Europe was also generous with her time, despite herself simultaneously preparing much more substantial Shakespearean projects. Like many of my colleagues in the Department of Coins and Medals, I regularly benefit from the skills and experience of Stephen Dodd, who is responsible for the images of numismatic material. I was delighted when Coralie Hepburn of BMCo suggested I write a book to coincide with the exhibition and working with the editor Claudia Bloch has been nothing but a pleasure.